LEGO® NEXO KNIGHTS™

WORLD OF NEXO KNIGHTS HEROES

OFFICIAL GUIDE

SCHOLASTIC INC.

The publisher does not have any control over and does not assume any responsibility for author or third-party websites or their content.

ISBN: 978-1-338-11412-6

10 9 8 7 6 5 4 3 2 1   17 18 19 20 21

Printed in the U.S.A.   40
First printing 2017

Book design by Rick DeMonico and Two Red Shoes Design

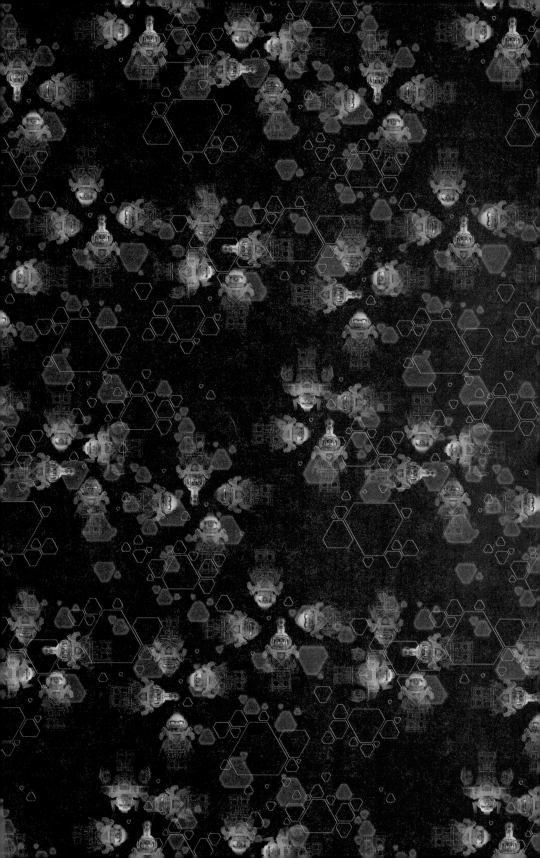

CONTENTS

INTRODUCTION:

UNLEASHING THE BOOK OF MONSTERS

Our story begins long, long ago in the kingdom of Knighton, when evil ruled the land and monsters ran free. For years, an evil wizard called Monstrox ruled over an army of magical monsters that terrorized all the good citizens of Knighton. Monstrox's ultimate goal: to take over the kingdom.

In order to stop Monstrox and bring much-needed peace to the kingdom, the royal wizard Merlok used sorcery to trap every evil spell and magical monster (and Monstrox himself) inside a collection of books. The wizard appointed himself the keeper of the books and for many years, Monstrox's nasty magic was hidden deep within Merlok's library.

But one of these books—the talking, evil-plan-hatching Book of Monsters—spent all that time coming up with a plan to escape Merlok's stuffy shelves and take over the Realm once and for all. Within The Book of Monster's pages lurked all of the most fearsome monsters the world had ever seen. In order to set those monsters free, the only thing The Book of Monsters needed was a sidekick. Someone who could wave a magic staff over the book's pages and bring the evil monsters back to life.

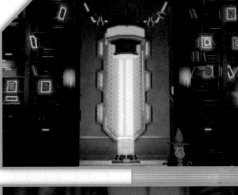

Enter Jestro, the court's jester . . .

Jestro was really bad at everything. He had unsuccessfully trained to be a knight. The poor guy wasn't even good at being a *jester*. His only friend was the newly graduated knight Clay Moorington. Everyone else in the kingdom laughed at him and called him a failure. After years of being laughed at, poor Jestro was sick and tired of people picking on him!

"I'm a horrible failure. I can't do anything right."
—Jestro

One day, after being humiliated in front of hundreds of people, Jestro slipped away from his royal duties and hid out in Merlok's library. In the cool, dark silence, surrounded by shelves of books, Jestro heard a voice calling to him. It was The Book of Monsters, who made an offer Jestro couldn't refuse. The Book of Monsters told Jestro that by waving a magic staff over the book's open pages, Jestro would become the ruler of an army of monsters so powerful *no one* would ever laugh at him again.

Finally, Jestro had a chance to prove he was good at something! It didn't take much for The Book of Monsters to convince Jestro this was his time to shine. After only a moment's thought, the court jester waved a staff over the pages of

the book and evil monsters sprang to life! Jestro had released his very own army of evil.

Of course, Jestro's old pal Clay and the other knights tried to fight back against Jestro and his monsters. But after a mighty battle, it was clear that muscle and iron is no match against magic. There was only one man who could fight off the magical creatures: Merlok. The wizard cast a mighty spell to try to stop the monsters. There was a huge, magical explosion . . .

The wizard's spell was so powerful that it blasted Jestro and The Book of Monsters to the other side of the Realm. The rest of the magical books—the very same ones that had been so carefully hidden in Merlok's library for all those years—were scattered to the far corners of the kingdom in the blast.

" I bet you could be good at being bad . . . I could make you the baddest baddie in the land."

–The Book of Monsters

And Merlok? At first, it seemed the wizard might be gone for good. But the king and his knights soon discovered that the wizard was not gone . . . he had just transformed. Merlok's own powerful spell had sucked him into the castle's computer system. He was no longer a flesh and blood wizard, but a glowing orange hologram. And the new Merlok 2.0 had special digital magic powers that he could use whenever and wherever he needed them!

After years of peace in the Realm, evil was once more on the loose. The good guys—Merlok and the brave NEXO KNIGHTS team—were determined to gather the books and destroy them. But The Book of Monsters and Jestro were eager to find them first so they could unleash even more evil magic on the kingdom. Whoever found the books first would have a great advantage in the battle of good versus evil. The race was on!

THE KNIGHTS OF KNIGHTON

Who can Knighton turn to when evil is on the loose? Knights, of course!

But in this land where magic and technology work together to keep the kingdom running smoothly, King Halbert relies on his extra-special Knights of Future Technology—the NEXO KNIGHTS team! Clay, Macy, Aaron, Axl, and Lance recently graduated from the Knights' Academy and still have a lot to learn, but now that The Book of Monsters is on the loose, they have been appointed as Knighton's official protectors. They are eager to do whatever it takes to protect the people of the Realm!

Of course, the five knights can't fight a whole army of magical monsters on their own. They have Merlok's digital magic on their side, a team of helpers, and a collection of very powerful weapons and vehicles to help them keep the kingdom safe. Introducing . . . your NEXO KNIGHTS heroes!

CLAY MOORINGTON

Clay is the most dedicated of all the knights. He works harder than anyone else on the team to ensure he is the best of the best. Everyone knows Clay takes his job *very* seriously. He graduated at the top of his class at the Knights' Academy, and he devotes his life to following the Knight's Code.

Clay loves coming up with training schedules and battle plans for the other knights (which never sits well with the rest of the team). He can be bossy, but he never gives up and is the most reliable of all the knights. Clay is definitely the knight you would want to come to your rescue if you were in trouble and needed a hero!

Knight Fast Facts

Weapon: Single-handed Claymore Sword

Signature Power: Stronghold of Resolution

Hometown: Dnullib—the smallest, dullest village in Knighton

Favorite Hobby: Self-improvement (he also loves trying to improve his fellow knights!). Clay can often be found watching and listening to instructional tapes from his favorite Knights' Academy instructors.

Quote: "I'm the only one here who truly lives by the Knight's Code!"

Greatest Fear: Fear of failure

Nothing is more frustrating to Clay than *not* being able to save the day!

There's only one thing Clay *isn't* good at: relaxing. So it's no surprise that the knights' unofficial leader was *not* pleased when the rest of the team sent him on vacation to buy themselves a much-needed break!

One of Clay's greatest honors came when he was given the chance to return to the Knights' Academy to help train the next generation of knights. But not long afterward, he faced the biggest challenge of his knighthood when wayward evil magic caused his body to begin to turn to stone. Trapped inside a body that no longer works the way it used to, Clay needs to rethink *everything* about himself and his role with the NEXO KNIGHTS team.

MACY HALBERT

MACY

Raised in the royal palace, surrounded by servants and tutors, Macy (the princess of Knighton) longs to be out on her own battling with the other knights. But Macy's father, King Halbert, expects his only child to take her job as princess very seriously. So Macy is often called away from her knightly duties to fulfill her royal duties, which annoys her *big time*. She just wants to swing her mace and jump into battles, not dress up in frilly dresses so she can smile and wave like a princess!

Even though she graduated second in her class (right behind Clay) at the Knights' Academy, Macy's father refused to honor Macy with her official NEXO shield on graduation day. Why? Because King Halbert believed Macy should learn to run the kingdom before she runs around fighting. Luckily, Queen Halbert was a great fighter back in her own day—so Macy borrowed her mom's shield and joined the knights . . . against her father's wishes.

Macy was extremely proud when she finally earned her father's respect—and was granted a shield of her own. As Macy fulfills her knightly duties, traveling around the Realm to prepare every town, village, and hamlet to be ready for monster attacks, she also learns some valuable lessons about what it takes to run a kingdom. Is it possible Macy can be both a NEXO KNIGHT hero and a powerful princess?

"Stop complaining—let's just kick some monster tail, old school!"

—Macy Halbert

Knight Fast Facts

Weapon: Power Mace

Signature Power: Rushing Strike

Hometown: The royal palace of Knighton

Favorite Hobby: When she isn't dreaming about or training to kick some monster tail, Macy loves reading comic books. Her role model is the famous knight, Ned Knightly, Man of Armor.

Quote: "The kingdom needs us, my father needs us. And I want to prove to him that I can be a knight, so badly."

Greatest Fear: Fear of not being able to fulfill her dream of being a NEXO KNIGHT hero

LANCE RICHMOND

Rich, handsome, famous, charming . . . *and* a NEXO KNIGHT hero? Lance has it *made*! Born into one of the richest families in the Realm, Lance can buy almost anything he wants—which means he is more than a little spoiled. Though Lance is a good guy at heart, he doesn't really know how to work hard, because he's never had to work for *anything*. He's spent his life surrounded by servants who will do anything for him—including his personal Squirebot butler, Dennis! Lance has even been known to pay someone to finish a fight for him if he's getting too sweaty.

"I call this look . . . Superstar!"

−Lance Richmond

Even though Lance always has the shiniest armor, loves partying in the trendiest knight clubs, and believes that relaxation and naps are the most important part of his training regimen, he longs to be a true hero. Though his leisure activities and acting career often distract him from his knightly duties, Lance eventually realizes that when he lifts a (well-manicured) finger and makes an effort, he is one of the best knights in the Realm.

Knight Fast Facts

Weapon: Lance

Signature Power: Thunder Blaze

Hometown: Auremville—the richest village in the kingdom

Favorite Hobbies: Relaxing, daily massages and nightly face masks, and hanging out with his pet pig, Hamletta

Quote: "Relaxation is an important part of my training regimen. The only part, really."

Greatest Fear: Fear of obscurity (Lance *hates* not being recognized.)

Lance's pet pig, Hamletta (Nickname: Sweetheart)

Did you know? Lance says he uses lavender body wash so he won't smell like a peasant!

AARON FOX

Atotal adrenaline junkie, Aaron is the most daring of all the knights. He loves speed, which means he often rushes into battle without a plan. Sometimes, this impulsiveness can get him into trouble, but many times Aaron's quick thinking can save the day!

Aaron doesn't always like to follow the rules or do things the *usual* way. In fact, as soon as Aaron got his shield from King Halbert, he figured out how to ride it like a hoverboard (which he's now dubbed his "*hover shield*"). Even though it bothers Clay when Aaron misuses his shield, this unconventional way of flying into battle definitely throws off his enemies. He also loves to strum his bow like he's playing an electric guitar—arrows fly out timed to the blasting beat when he's using his bow in "Music Mode"!

If Aaron ever figures out how to plan ahead and keeps his daredevil spirit under control (by tapping into his wild side only when it doesn't endanger others) there could be a bigger role for him to play in the knights' future . . .

Knight Fast Facts

Weapon: Blazer Bow

Signature Power: Swift Sting

Hometown: Grindstead—a seaside fishing village with a beach-bum lifestyle

Favorite Hobby: Knightkour—Aaron loves using the whole kingdom as his own personal obstacle course for running, jumping, and climbing over things!

Quote: "I got my hover shield. Only ride I need!"

Greatest Fear: Fear of having nothing to do

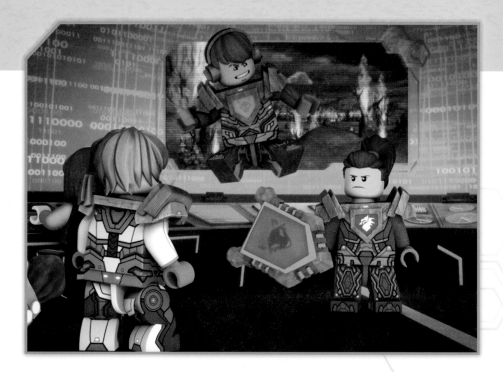

"I have to do *nothing* for a whole ten minutes?!"

—Aaron Fox

AXL

Axl is a gentle giant whose greatest asset is his brute force strength. He's *huge* and strong, but it takes a lot of food to keep this guy's energy up. He's the most powerful of all the knights . . . and also the hungriest. Axl is kind, gentle, and patient when he needs to be, but when he gets angry (or *hangry*) he will mash, smash, peel, and julienne his enemies.

Axl is strong enough to lift and move just about anything. In fact, he developed his strength as a kid by moving rocks from a very young age.

He feels most at home in the hills—and in the kitchen. When he's not mashing monsters, Axl loves to cook, and he uses his axe to mash potatoes and chop vegetables. After studying with Chef Éclair, the knights' cook-bot, Axl gains fame as the Realm's biggest—well, *only*—singing chef! Could Axl's appetite for performing ever get in the way of his duties as a NEXO KNIGHT hero?

Knight Fast Facts

Weapon: Power Axe

Signature Power: Raging Rally

Hometown: Diggington—located in the northern Hill Country, where no one needs a last name

Favorite Hobbies: Eating, cooking, and strumming the electric lute in his band, the Boogie Knights

Quote: "I baked a cake in your honor . . . and then I ate it in your honor."

Greatest Fear: Fear of hunger

"I'm hungry . . . for action!"

—Axl

The Making of a Knight:
KNIGHTS' ACADEMY

"Ut Ad Arma, Atque Ad Protegendum!"
Learning to Shield and to Protect!

Most kids in Knighton grow up dreaming of becoming a knight. So where do young hopefuls go to learn the tricks of the trade? The Knights' Academy! At the academy, students attend classes and learn from the best of the best.

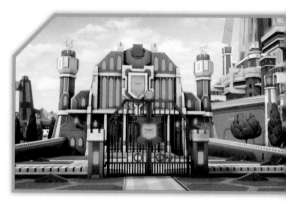

Highlights of the Knights' Academy Coursework

YEAR ONE—Novice
- Introduction to the Knight's Code: Basics of Knighthood
- Chivalry and Ethics 101
- Combat Skills
- Castle Economics

YEAR TWO—Apprentice
- The History of Knighton
- Combat Skills
- Technology
- Woodwork and Forest Monsters

YEAR THREE—Weapon Bearer
- Geography of Knighton
- Diplomacy/Debate
- Introduction to Monsters
- Physical Education

YEAR FOUR—Squire
- Advanced Monsters
- History of the Royal Families of Knighton
- Posing Heroically
- Field Study

When they've completed their training, students receive a Knights' Academy Degree of Knighthood and are awarded their Knight's Shield. Only then are they declared Shield Bearers and become official Protectors of the Realm.

As soon as they arrive at the academy, each young knight-in-training receives a copy of *The Knight's Code* to help inspire them. The ancient guidebook is one of the most important documents studied and learned at the Knights' Academy (as Clay tends to remind the team again . . . and again . . . and again).

Some of the most powerful magic books in the Realm are shelved in the different libraries at the Knights' Academy.

Librarian:
Persnickity Marge

THE KNIGHTS' ALLIES

MERLOK 2.0

Merlok 2.0 is the NEXO KNIGHTS team's mentor. He helps the knights learn how to use their NEXO Powers and high-tech weapons to overcome evil monsters. Merlok can use spells, enchanted objects, and wizard weapons . . . and he knows more about illusion and magic than anyone else in the Realm.

"Isn't magic just the best?!"

—Merlok 2.0

When Merlok cast the powerful spell that blasted Jestro and The Book of Monsters to the farthest reaches of the kingdom, he was sucked into a computer program. He's now a digital hologram that lives inside the Operating System for the Fortrex, a rolling castle that is home base for the knights. While he knows a lot, he's very scatterbrained as a result of being a hologram, leading to some humorous results. The "Wizard of the OS" can download an amazing array of digital magic weapons and powers to the knights through their shields.

Long before Clay, Macy, Aaron, Lance, or Axl were born, Merlok used sorcery to split the evil Monstrox into twelve Books of Evil. He hoped this would keep the kingdom safe from monsters. This spell worked for over one hundred years . . . until the day Jestro waved a magic staff over The Book of Monsters and brought evil back to life!

AVA PRENTIS & ROBIN UNDERWOOD:
Junior Knights of the Realm

Ava Prentis and Robin Underwood are still knights-in-training—but they're an essential part of the NEXO KNIGHTS team. Though they are enrolled in their second year at the Knights' Academy, they can most often be found traveling around in the Fortrex with the knights. These two eager young knights-in-training have discovered it's *much* more fun to learn on the job, though they still sometimes teach classes and workshops at the academy.

It took some time, but after Robin and Ava proved their worth to the NEXO KNIGHTS team, King Halbert recognized them as official junior knights of the Realm.

Ava is a technology wiz. She's a genius when it comes to anything electronic, especially computers. Ava is actually the one who found Merlok inside the castle's computer system, and she handles all programming for the team. She keeps the high-tech NEXO Power systems running, was heavily involved in creating Combo NEXO Powers, and she serves as Merlok 2.0's apprentice.

Robin is the knights' builder and designer. The son of the castle's former maintenance man, Robin loves creating new gadgets, armor, and weapons. He's the guy the whole team turns to when they need their gear fixed or upgraded.

"I'm a doer, not a studier."
–Robin Underwood

Robin is constantly trying to prove he's ready to be a full knight. In fact, shortly after he joined the team as a knight-in-training, Robin built Battle Mech—"The Black Knight"—to try to prove to the knights that he should be a full member of the team! Though he's still enrolled in the Knights' Academy, he's doing a yearlong independent study project with Merlok 2.0, helping the wizard with many secret projects.

Some of Robin and Ava's most important inventions include: the team's Battle Suits and vehicles, Ultra Armor, and the Triangulator (a special device used for testing and combining NEXO Powers).

Battle Suits

The Triangulator

KING AND QUEEN HALBERT

Born into royalty, King Halbert is not a warrior by nature; he would much rather be a peacetime king. The king's favorite activities are talking to people, hosting tournaments, and attending parties and royal functions. Despite the fact that he's not big on battle, he *can* stand up for himself and his people . . . especially if he's using his trusty Royal Mech!

Though he doesn't like fighting, King Halbert *loves* the special Battle Suit Robin built for him to use in an epic battle against Jestro and The Book of Monsters. This sleek robotic suit is equipped with state-of-the-art technology, such as a holovisor, a flying shield, and a double-edged power sword. When he realizes how much fun it is to wear, the king does *everything* in his beloved Mech: attends inaugurations, performs ceremonies, and even sleeps and eats in it!

Because he loves his wife and daughter and would do anything possible to keep them safe, King Halbert would much rather see Macy focus on her royal duties than be a member of the NEXO KNIGHTS team. He hopes someday Macy will take over the throne and become the queen of Knighton . . . but after watching her fight, King Halbert realizes his daughter is much more like her mother: a warrior, a knight, and unhappy being kept on the sidelines.

The king uses chainmail to communicate with Macy and the other knights while they're on the road.

"Your mace-work makes your mama proud!"

–Queen Halbert

Queen Hama Halbert was born a commoner. Because of this, she is very down-to-earth and beloved by the people of the Realm. When the king first met her, she was serving as a warrior in a village. Their marriage is proof that opposites attract! The queen hopes Macy will follow in her mother's footsteps as a warrior . . . this is part of the reason she gave Macy her old shield!

SQUIREBOTS OF KNIGHTON

Squirebots are the little robots that help keep Knighton running smoothly. They fill many roles: soldiers in battle, servants, reporters, chefs, mechanics . . . the list goes on and on! For almost any task that needs to be done, there is a Squirebot that can handle it. In Knighton, a Squirebot is a knight's best friend.

SQUIREBOTS OF NOTE:

Dennis is Lance's trusty servant and personal butler.

Squirazzi follow celebrities—like Lance!—around with cameras.

Haute Fancypants is the king's special assistant. He acts as an advisor, greets dignitaries, and takes care of many other important duties for the king.

Chef Éclair keeps the knights well fed in their rolling Fortrex— and even takes time out of his busy schedule to train Axl as a chef!

KNIGHTS IN TRAINING

There are plenty of hopeful knights-in-training at the Knights' Academy who would be happy to jump in and help the NEXO KNIGHTS team if they needed backup!

All students at the Knights' Academy work hard to impress Principal Brickland.

Izzy Richmond (Lance's sister!) and Fletch Bowman are two promising young students at the Knights' Academy.

KNIGHTON CELEBRITIES

Drumroll please! Introducing some of Knighton's most famous citizens (other than Lance, of course!) . . .

Gobbleton Rambley is a celebrity chef.

Edvard Edvardson is the snobby curator of the king's fine art museum.

Jorah Tightwad and his Tighty Knighties (Jousting Beeber, Brickney Spears, Shia LaBlade, and The Blok). Though Jorah is a rival royal to King Halbert, he's not a bad guy—just a big fan of fame and fortune!

Sir Griffiths is the mysterious knight who used to work with Merlok.

THE FORTREX

This moving castle rolls across the land and serves as the NEXO KNIGHTS team's headquarters, as well as being the home base of the Merlok 2.0 Operating System. Once a mobile vacation home for the royal family—affectionately known as Ye Olde Royal RV—the Fortrex is now a self-contained rolling battle fortress that is outfitted with everything the knights need while they're protecting the land!

Sleeping quarters with massage beds

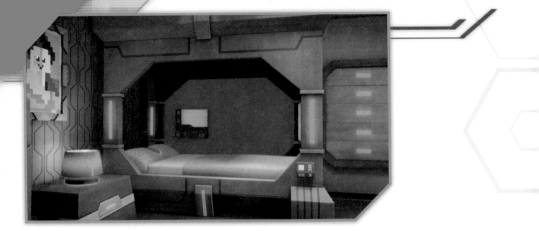

A fully equipped armory and state-of-the-art training area. The hologym lets the knights hone their skills in simulated towns and battle arenas.

A kitchen run by Chef Éclair, the team's cook-bot

A library and computer room for studying, as well as a downtime area for video games and relaxing

EQUIPMENT & WEAPONS

Every high-tech knight needs a powerful suit of armor to protect his or her body in battle. The knights' armor often has NEXO Power flowing through it, which gives the wearer extra strength and protection. Even better, the knights' armor can be equipped with upgrades that give the knights even more of an edge when they're fighting monsters!

KNIGHTS' ARMOR

As the knights' needs and enemies change, Robin works hard to outfit the team with cutting-edge armor that keeps them protected.

First, Robin hooked the knights up with Ultra Armor . . .

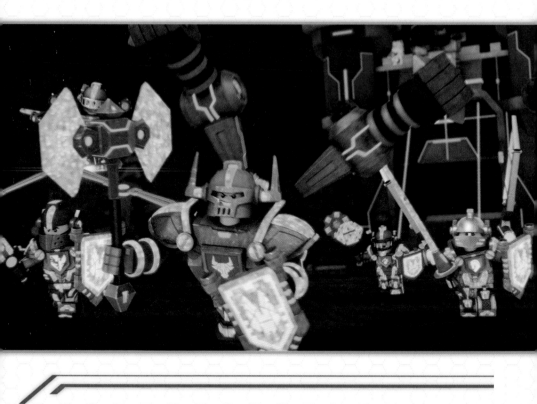

Shortly afterward, Robin developed the Black Knight Mech for *himself* to use . . .

. . . and the Black Knight Mech paved the way for Robin's latest creation: Battle Suits. The NEXO KNIGHTS team's Battle Suits are smaller, sleeker, high-tech versions of the Black Knight Mech. The coolest thing about Battle Suits? They allow a single knight to wield a Combo NEXO Power.

KNIGHTS' SHIELDS

In the Realm of Knighton, a shield is a knight's most personal possession because it displays the individual's family crest. It is also a badge of excellence, honor, and pride . . . and oftentimes a real lifesaver, since a knight's shield protects him or her against attacks! The NEXO KNIGHTS team's shields are a lot like traditional shields, except that they are equipped with Wi–Fi and a digital screen for downloading NEXO Powers!

WEAPONS

Every knight has a favorite weapon, whether it's a sword, a lance, a bow and arrow, a power axe, or a mace.

Clay favors a single-handed Claymore Sword with a double-edged blade. His signature sword is nearly as tall as him and super heavy, too!

Axl's Power Axes aren't just useful for crushing and slicing monsters on the battlefield—he also uses his signature weapon for cooking!

Lance's high-tech, expensive collection of lances keeps monsters at bay—and most have a flared hilt at the bottom of the blade. Lance has been known to call "time-out" in the middle of battle, and balance on top of his lance.

Aaron owns several variations of his signature Blazer Bow, all of which have energy bolts that release when the trigger is pulled!

Each of Macy's powered-up Photon Maces can send monsters scurrying—and they also deflect incoming missiles!

So how do you destroy a magic monster? Even the slightest touch from a NEXO-Powered weapon will send any monster back to the book from which it was summoned. But to destroy a Stone Monster, the knights must use three powers together for a Combo NEXO Power! More on that on the next few pages . . .

NEXO POWERS

Basic weapons and armor are essential for jousting or fighting ordinary enemies, but they don't do much against magical monsters. That's where NEXO Powers come into play! So what exactly *are* NEXO Powers? They are a fusion of digital technology and magic that power the knights' shields and weapons with awesome monster-fighting capabilities.

The knights' shields work a lot like traditional shields, but they are even more powerful and protective. Thanks to his digital magic, Merlok 2.0 can upload just the right NEXO Power to the knights via their shields. When a knight gets into trouble, he or she just holds his or her shield high in the air to download a power upgrade . . .

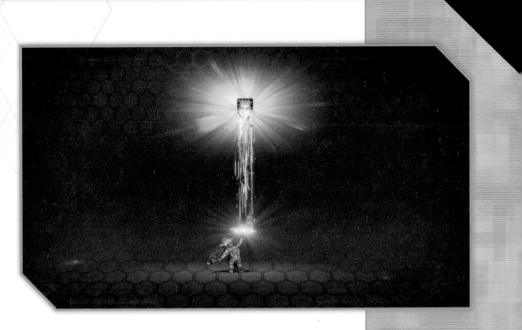

The knight feels the rush of energy as the power is channeled from his or her shield through to his or her armor and weapons . . .

Once he or she is powered up, the knight's armor and weapons glow!

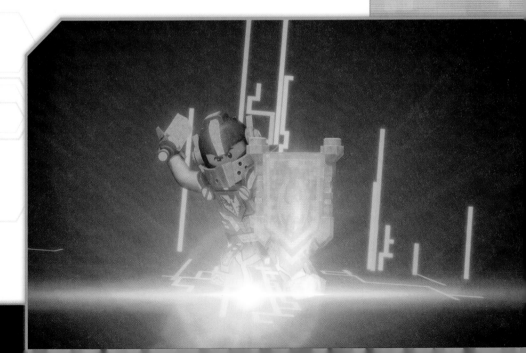

So what do you do when regular NEXO Powers aren't *enough*? If you're Robin and Ava, you come up with the next generation of NEXO Powers . . .

COMBO NEXO POWERS!

Combo NEXO Powers only work if a knight is wearing a Battle Suit . . . or if three knights work together! These mega NEXO Powers are the only thing that can shatter the Cloud of Monstrox's Stone Monsters.

In a monster fight, Merlok 2.0 can download just the right NEXO Powers to the knights. He figures out exactly what the knights need to defeat a foe, then provides his team with the perfect NEXO Power to combat it. But Combo NEXO Powers are still experimental—Merlok 2.0 doesn't always get them right, which leads to some hilarious results!

VEHICLES FIT FOR A KNIGHT

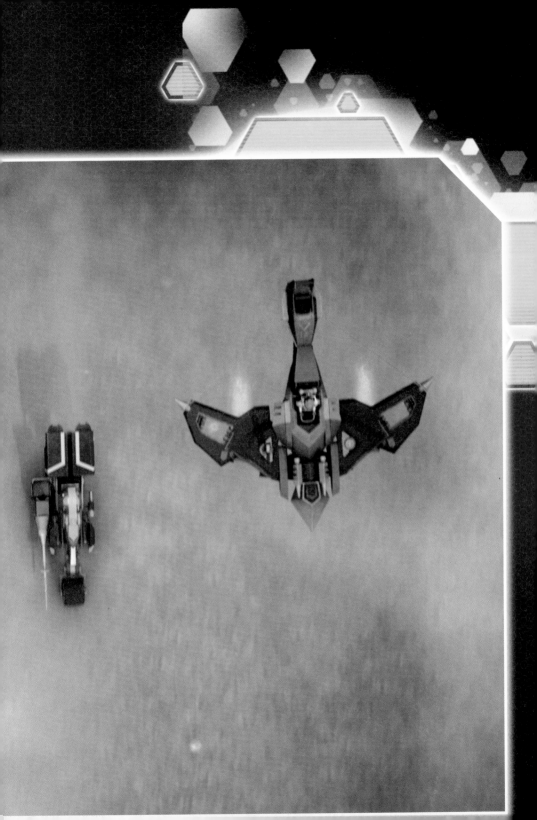

CLAY'S RUMBLE BLADE

As the knights' skills and responsibilities have evolved over time, Robin has ensured that each of their signature vehicles are upgraded to fit the team's changing needs. Because they're knights, each member of the team has a customized hover horse . . . but they often charge into battles in their own one-of-a-kind vehicles that suit each of their styles perfectly!

Clay's Rumble Blade is a six-wheeled tank with a sword-shaped front. Best of all, the Rumble Blade is actually four tough machines in one—with dozens of cool features that help Clay kick some monster tail:

The Rumble Base is a three-wheeled vehicle with two high-power rear wheels that tear through rough terrain. Two Sword Break Bikes—usually piloted by loyal Clay Bots—can break away from the Rumble Blade and hurtle into battle. A speedy Blade Flyer detaches from the top of the Rumble Blade to whisk Clay off the ground so he can fight his foes in midair.

AARON'S HOVER SHIELD AND AERO STRIKER

Aaron's shield doesn't just protect him in battle. He also customized it to work as a "hover shield" which can zip around the Realm in style.

Aaron's Aero Striker lets this adrenaline junkie fly through the air at seriously intense speeds. It is equipped with multiple missiles that Aaron and his Squirebot copilot can fire at foes.

LANCE'S MECHA HORSE AND TURBO STRIKER

Lance's high-tech horse is *all* style . . . a Richmond expects nothing less than the best! The metal beast—which Lance has named Concordo—has a shiny blue coat and can even transform into a low-riding Turbo Striker motorcycle!

Concordo in cycle form

MACY'S SPEEDER AND MACE SLAMMER

Princess Macy is always ready to roll—into action!—in her Thunder Mace. Macy's vehicle has flip-up rotating cannons and a hardcore front wheel that allows her to go almost anywhere.

Because there are times when Macy needs a smaller, speedier vehicle, Robin built her a miniature, high-flying Mace Slammer. It has armored wings, a jet engine, and just enough room for Macy in the cockpit.

AXL'S
TOWER CARRIER

riginally designed to safely transport magic books, Axl's hulking Tower Carrier rises over almost everything on a battlefield. When Axl needs a second vehicle, the Battle Tower can break away from the carrier to create a mobile battle station. The hidden catapult inside the tower can swivel, and even folds out when the tower is removed from the base!

BAD GUYS & MONSTERS

So where have all these monsters been kept for the past one hundred years? Inside The Book of Monsters! To release them, Jestro waves the magic staff he stole from Merlok's library over a page in the book and POOF! Instant monsters!

JESTRO

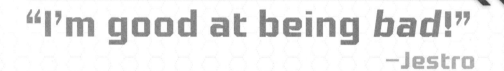

Jestro hasn't always been a bad guy. For a long time, he was King Halbert's court jester and he tried so, so hard to be good. But nobody ever laughed at Jestro's jokes, and his juggling routines were always a big flop. Jestro grew tired of being a laughingstock. He was desperate to succeed at *something*. So when The Book of Monsters suggested they partner up, Jestro decided to give being mean a chance. As soon as he released a few monsters, Jestro realized just how good it felt to be *bad*.

"I'm good at being *bad!*"
—Jestro

Jestro took his mission—to find and collect all the other Books of Evil—very seriously . . . because he believed The Book of Monsters when he promised Jestro that he might someday rule all of Knighton with a magical iron fist! But Jestro eventually realized The Book of Monsters had been playing him for a fool (not the good kind), and the former jester began to regret his evil ways. He even tried to help the knights stop The Book of Monsters!

Unfortunately, Jestro's plan to stick to a life less evil went awry when the Cloud of Monstrox zapped him with a nasty bolt of lightning and dragged him back to the bad side. And this time, the plan isn't to take over the Realm . . . now, Jestro and Monstrox want to destroy it!

"Wave the staff over the page and you get a monster!"
—The Book of Monsters

THE BOOK OF MONSTERS

"Turn the page . . . find another monster!"

–The Book of Monsters

The Book of Monsters is much more than a book filled with magical monsters. It can talk, think, and bring monsters to life. What's worse, every time Jestro and the crew find another Book of Dark Magic, The Book of Monsters gobbles it down whole . . . and the monsters on the book's pages grow even more powerful. But whenever the knights *defeat* a monster, the bad guy gets sent back into the book. *Buuurp!*

"Nobody betrays me, joke-boy, nobody."
–The Book of Monsters

Bookkeeper: This small monster—with arms and legs—was conjured up with a wave of Jestro's magic staff after the evil jester got tired of hauling the big Book of Monsters around. Now the Bookkeeper does the heavy lifting!

Did you know?
The Bookkeeper really knows how to enjoy his rare days off!

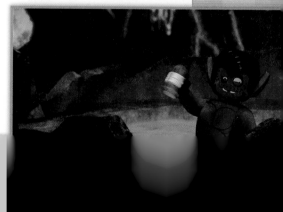

THE CLOUD OF MONSTROX

More than one hundred years ago, Monstrox was the evil wizard that plagued Knighton. He created and commanded an army of vicious monsters until Merlok tricked him and trapped him inside a magic book. Stuck as The Book of Monsters, Monstrox plotted his revenge and came up with a plan to rule again.

Now that The Book of Monsters has returned to his former glory as Monstrox—though his spirit is now trapped inside a lightning-filled cloud—this evil sorcerer can bring stone to life with his magical lightning.

With a rock-solid army at his disposal, the Cloud of Monstrox begins a quest to find the Forbidden Powers that Merlok stole from him long ago. If Monstrox and Jestro can collect enough of the Forbidden Powers, they will be able to bring the huge Stone Colossus to life and destroy Knighton once and for all.

Jestro feels *extra* powerful wielding the Staff of Monstrox.

MAGMA MONSTERS

Magma Monsters are made of hot liquid rock that is boiling over with evil! Here are a few of the most important members of Jestro's army:

Globlins, Bloblins, and Scurriers: Hundreds of these little beasts populate Jestro's monster armies. Globlins are little bouncing fireballs that bounce around and excel at mass attacks. If a bunch of Globlins mash together, they form Bloblins that can breathe fireballs. Speedy Scurriers have arms and legs and love to scurry around, menacing their opponents.

After these little pests catch a bug in Snottingham, they turn into Sickness monsters!

Burnzie and Sparkks: Not the brightest pair of monsters, Burnzie (the horned beast) and his best pal, Sparkks (the one-eyed warrior), are constantly getting destroyed by the knights . . . but they keep coming back to try to prove themselves.

General Magmar: This evil warlord was once the right-hand man and army commander for Monstrox. He's been cooped up inside The Book of Monsters for far too long, and when he finally gets out he proves he's one bad dude.

Whiparella: This nasty villain with a snakelike body can find your fears . . . then with the snaps of her whips, all your worst nightmares come to life. Even Jestro is terrified of Whiparella!

Lavaria: Keep your mouth shut around this super-spy, because she can't be trusted. The Monster Army's best spy is stealthy, sneaky, and has a unique ability to use boiling hot magma as a weapon!

The Beast Master: Produced by
The Book of Chaos, the Beast Master is
a top-notch monster wrangler. He has the
unique ability to turn a bunch of small monsters
into a mass of controlled destruction!

Moltor and Flama: These twin brothers are complete
opposites. Flama is a molten mass of liquid lava, while Moltor
is a bashing, boulder-fisted rock of a monster. They love
combining their skills to cause double trouble.

STONE MONSTERS

Brought to life with a single lightning zap from the Cloud of Monstrox, this stone army is a force to be reckoned with . . . luckily, the NEXO KNIGHTS heroes are up to the challenge!

Stone Colossus:
A huge stone monster that was once Mount Thunderstrox, brought to life by Jestro and the Cloud of Monstrox

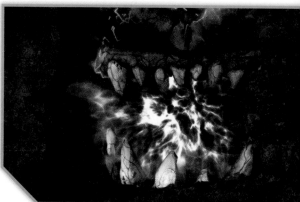

Gargoyles: Gargoyles used to be nothing more than ornamental statues perched atop towers in the city of Ghoulia. But now that they have been zapped to life, they're Monstrox's eager servants.

General Garg: Made from blackened granite, the leader of the Gargoyles is as grumpy as he looks!

Stone Stompers: These living stone statues often resemble knights.

Bouldrons: These round stone beasts with spikes will roll, hop, and bounce everywhere they're not wanted!

Gravellers: Gravellers are smaller and less spiky than Bouldrons, but just as annoying!

Pebblers: These speedy little Stone Monsters have arms, legs, *and* horns.

Stone Gnomes: These menacing little critters with pointy hats will poke at you with a vengeance.

Harpies: Ulrika, Hilda, and Ingrid are three sister gargoyles who favor air attacks—thanks to their electrified wings!

Roguls: The Roguls are supposed to be guarding the Forbidden Powers, but now they're saturated with the dark magic, and anything they come into contact with will be affected.

Grimrocks: Found in the petrified forest of Rock Wood, these big beasts were Monstrox's original warriors, back in the day. They're baaaaack . . . and harder and heavier than ever!

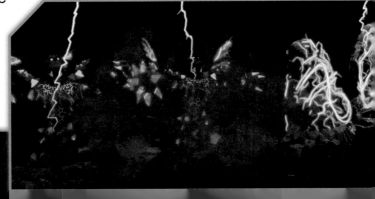

The Three Brothers:

Reex, Roog, and Rumble are three granite golems that were dug up from under a mountain. They come in three handy sizes to meet all of Monstrox's Stone Monsters needs: mini, regular, and BIG.

Roberto Arnoldi:

This famous artist creates statues which are brought to life and called into Jestro's service.

Ruina Stoneheart:

This mysterious witch possesses powerful magic, and may be hiding a very *big* secret!

VEHICLES OF EVIL

The enemies of the NEXO KNIGHTS heroes have their own ways of getting around, using some pretty strange means of transportation . . .

Evil Mobile:

Jestro traveled across the kingdom in his own rolling fortress called the Evil Mobile (which has since been retired). It is outfitted with giant lava wheels, two catapults, and a hidden trap ladder.

The Beast Master's Chariot:

The Beast Master's chariot is drawn by two giant Globlins and has a catapult at the back!

Machine of Doom:

General Magmar's pride and joy is his Siege Machine of Doom. It is jammed full of weapons and missiles, has hubcaps made of flaming spikes, and can even flip up to give the general an even better view of the battlefield. It's a vehicle and a siege tower in one!

Evil Headquarters:

After the Evil Mobile was rusted out of existence, Jestro and the Cloud of Monstrox enlisted Roberto Arnoldi to create them a mobile base of operations—the Evil Headquarters!

BOOKS OF EVIL

For years, this collection of evil magic books was locked safely away in Merlok's library. But now they are scattered all over Knighton. When the NEXO KNIGHTS team's quest begins, The Book of Monsters is on the hunt—if he can collect them all, he will be able to bring Monstrox back to life! Can the knights find them before The Book of Monsters swallows them all?

> "We'll find more and more magic books and get stronger and stronger until nobody can stop us!"
>
> —The Book of Monsters

The Book of Evil: Jestro perfects his evil laugh when he finds his first nasty book.

The Book of Chaos:
When Jestro and The Book of Monsters find this book in an old ruin, chaos reigns across the Realm!

The Book of Fear:
With this book in Jestro's control, everyone's greatest fears are brought into focus (including Jestro's own worst fear of being a laughingstock!).

The Book of Anger:
No good can come when raging anger takes hold!

The Book of Deception:
Jestro uses this book—the only evil book that can create fake copies of itself!—to turn his army of evil into clones of the "goody-goody" knights!

The Book of Destruction:

Destroying worlds is this book's specialty—it even has the potential to destroy the entire kingdom.

The Book of Revenge:

Got a grudge? The Book of Revenge will help you get back at your enemies!

The Book of Greed:

All good people are overcome by greed when they're in the company of this bad book.

The Book of Envy:

Jestro snags this book—with the power to make its keeper desire all their neighbors' stuff—from Jorah Tightwad and his Tighty Knighties.

The Book of Cruelty:

This cruel tome was hidden inside the hotel the knights sent Clay to for a relaxing weekend, with very funny consequences.

The Book of Betrayal:

Jestro's hero— funnyman Jokes Knightly—used the book to trick people into thinking his stolen jokes were funny.

FORBIDDEN POWERS

The Forbidden Powers are destructive spells that were outlawed by the Wizards' Council and sealed in stone tablets by Merlok long ago. These tablets were then hidden all over the kingdom, safely kept in special statues called Roguls. Over time, the Forbidden Powers began to seep out of their stone hiding spots, affecting the areas around them—this has started to provide clues about where they might be found!

Jestro and the Cloud of Monstrox are on a quest to find each of the Forbidden Powers. Their hope: that they might awaken the giant Stone Colossus. In order to do this, Jestro and the Cloud of Monstrox must:

► Locate a Forbidden Power.
► Zap the Rogul to life and release the Forbidden Power.
► Jestro then inserts the Forbidden Power into the Staff of Monstrox so he can wield the power.
► After infusing their Stone Army with the Power, Jestro needs to transfer all the Forbidden Powers to the standing stones atop Mount Thunderstrox as soon as possible.

The first four Forbidden Powers that Jestro and the Cloud of Monstrox find and collect are:

Relentless Rust:

This power gives them the ability to instantly rust everything they come into contract with, rendering vehicles and weapons useless!

Ravaging Rot:

This power really stinks . . . with Ravaging Rot, the baddies can make everything that grows in the kingdom—vegetables, fruit, trees—rot and fester.

Crippling Crumble:

This power causes rock, stone, and other structures to crumble to dust.

Blazing Burn:

This ultra-hot power can set anything on fire . . . when they gain control of it, Jestro and the Cloud of Monstrox hope to burn the entire kingdom to the ground.

THE KINGDOM OF KNIGHTON

The Realm of Knighton is filled with cities, towns, villages, forests, and distant lands. The knights are charged with defending the entire kingdom from evil. They travel far and wide, protecting the citizens in dozens of small, peaceful hamlets like this one:

Knightonia: The largest city in the Realm is home to the royal family and the Knights' Academy.

Holo-Wood: Lance makes his Holo-Wood acting debut in the movie *The Golden Castle*!

The Hill Country: Axl's hometown of Diggington is in the mountainous, mine-filled northernmost part of the Realm.

Did you know?

Axl's mom also loves to cook. Axl loves her porcupine stew!

Auremville: This is the region of Knighton where Lance comes from. The Richmond family is beloved in this region that has streets paved with gold and marble, and Lance's parents' gold castle sits at the center of everything.

Bookingham: Home of the Knight-a-Con Conference

Pepperton: Home of the Pepperton Chili Cook-off

Cleanington: The cleanest village in the Realm

Snottingham: Coldest town in Knighton

Funnyton: Hiding place of The Book of Betrayal

WHERE EVIL LURKS

Lava Lands: This fiery realm—the *hottest* real estate in Knighton—is where the bad guys hang out.

Jestro's Volcano Lair: Located in the heart of the Lava Lands—nestled among active volcanos, geysers, and steaming lava—Jestro plots and schemes in Monstrox's former castle.

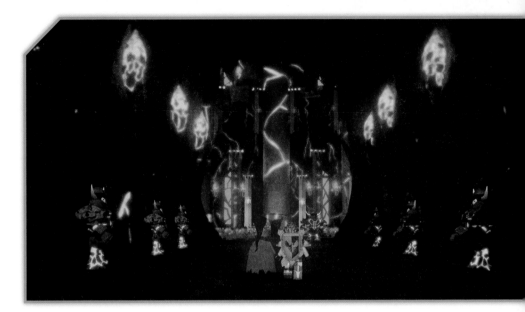

The Dark Arena: One of the many scary rooms inside Jestro's headquarters

Mount Thunderstrox: High atop this mountain, Monstrox seeks to unite the Forbidden Powers in order to unleash the Stone Colossus.

Swamp Castle: This nasty, evil castle is surrounded by a fetid, rotting, stinking swamp.

Ghoulia: This gothic city that is filled with Gargoyles is the perfect place for Jestro and the Cloud of Monstrox to zap their new army to life.

The Iron Mountains: These once stony mountains are now rusty because the Forbidden Power of Relentless Rust was kept there for many years.

Rock Wood: Back in the day, Merlok defeated Monstrox in this petrified forest. With one mighty spell, the entire forest and army of monsters was turned to stone.

HERE'S THE LATEST FROM THE KNIGHTON NEWS NETWORK!

This is Herb Herbertson and Alice Squires, bringing you the latest from the Knighton News Network. If you've missed *any* of the thrilling action around Knighton, read on for the highlights!

On graduation day, all our newly graduated NEXO KNIGHTS heroes were awarded their family shields . . . except Princess Macy. *Ouch!*

Our once-peaceful kingdom was rocked when Jestro stole the terrible Book of Monsters!

The Book of Fear unleashed Whiparella . . . and exposed the NEXO KNIGHTS team's darkest nightmares!

Knight-in-training Robin Underwood created the Black Knight to defeat Jestro's crew . . . and try to prove his worth to the NEXO KNIGHTS team!

The knights were all held hostage by Jestro's evil army! But thanks to airborne archer Aaron, they managed to escape . . .

. . . just in time to fight back as Jestro and The Book of Monsters stormed the king's castle!

In an epic battle of good versus evil, even King Halbert got in on the action in his all-new, state-of-the-art Royal Mech!

Everyone in the kingdom breathed a sigh of relief when the knights won and Princess Macy finally got the shield she deserved.

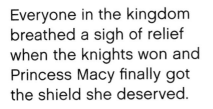

When the knights headed back to visit the academy, they stopped in for a visit with Principal Brickland and the grouchy librarian, Persnickity Marge.

Uh-oh! Jestro went back to school, too—and stole Librarian Marge's magical snow globe.

Turns out, Monstrox's old castle was trapped inside the snow globe! Now, it's Jestro's new headquarters in the Lava Lands.

At a royal banquet, the knights faced off against Jorah Tightwad and his Tighty Knighties to try to win The Book of Envy.

Though the Tighty Knighties put on a good show, they had to be saved by the NEXO KNIGHTS team!

When the knights visited Snottingham, they walked away with much more than they bargained for. The knights can't fight when their NEXO Powers catch a cold . . .

It wasn't funny when Jokes Knightly—Jestro's comic hero—got his hands on The Book of Betrayal.

The knights managed to snag The Book of Betrayal after Jestro betrayed The Book of Monsters. Merlok 2.0 knew his team needed to protect this book extra-carefully, since it was the last evil book not in The Book of Monster's control!

But as usual, The Book of Monsters had a plan . . . for Jestro *and* for getting his foul teeth on the last book. "When this ceremony is over . . . *you'll be Monstrox!*" —The Book of Monsters

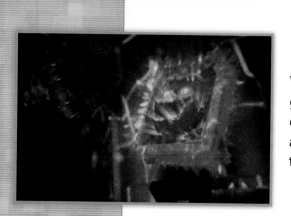

When The Book of Monsters gained control of the Book of Deception, he was finally able to bring Monstrox back to life!

After the Cloud of Monstrox formed, it immediately began to cast its shadow on the Realm.

And the NEXO KNIGHTS heroes needed to figure out a different way to fight their newest foes . . . *Stone Monsters!*

While zapping a statue with his evil power, Monstrox hit Clay with one of his blasts— and something strange happened to the knights' leader . . .

Evil took another step forward when the first Forbidden Power was put into place in the Standing Stones atop Mount Thunderstrox.

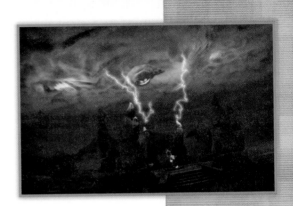

With Clay turned completely into a granite statue, who will lead the knights now?!

As Colossus's face appears in the side of the mountain, Monstrox grew more powerful than ever. "He will soon come to life and we will use it to lay waste to this land!"—Monstrox

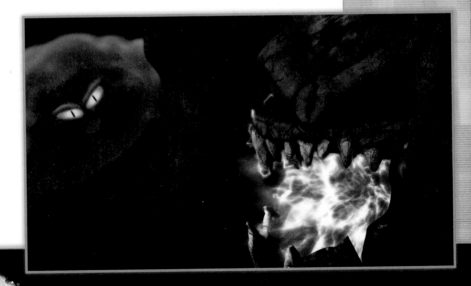

A GLIMPSE INTO THE FUTURE

Things are looking dire in the fine kingdom of Knighton . . .

Clay has turned completely to stone and, despite the fact that Aaron has been working with Clay and Merlok to take on more responsibilities, the team seems leaderless. After Merlok's deep memory was fried by a hit from Monstrox, Ava had to rebuild him from the ground up. Meanwhile, Jestro has already located four of the Forbidden Powers and put them into the Standing Stones atop Mount Thunderstrox—which, in turn, helped the Cloud of Monstrox grow bigger and more powerful than ever before.

   Even though the whole kingdom of Knighton is down and out, the NEXO KNIGHTS heroes aren't prepared to give up without a fight . . .

Read on for a sneak peek from
The Gray Knight!

"C'mon, c'mon!" The Cloud of Monstrox bellowed at Jestro. "I'm feeling so totally recharged that I'm laser-focused on finding that next Forbidden Power. Oh! Oh! I think that's it!"

Jestro steered the Evil Headquarters around a corner. His face lit up when he spotted an old statue—a Rogul—hidden inside an outcropping of rocks. "Yes! Another Forbidden Power! What is it, Cloudy?"

"Shocking Scare!" The Cloud of Monstrox cried. "This will turn even the bravest hero into a whimpering coward."

Jestro gave his partner a funny look. "How is *that* destructive?"

"Uh . . ." The Cloud of Monstrox considered this. "It, uh, destroys . . . courage! Yeah, yeah—that's good. Now let's unlock this power."

Jestro watched from a safe distance as the cloud zapped the statue with a bolt of lightning. As soon as the magical blast hit the statue, the solid stone Rogul came to life. Jestro approached the statue and grabbed the tablet containing the Forbidden Power. He locked it into the Staff of Monstrox and grinned. "Let's try this baby out!"

With the Cloud of Monstrox looking on from above, Jestro waved the staff in front of the Rogul. The statue shrieked, turned away, and cowered before Jestro in fear.

"Oh yeah!" The Cloud of Monstrox whooped. "Scaring a Rogul is no easy feat. This Power is frightfully good."

Jestro nodded. "Back to the Rolling HQ . . . it's time to try my new power out!"

"Sounds good." The Cloud of Monstrox released

an evil laugh. "Since I zapped Merlok's memory of the Forbidden Powers, he probably doesn't remember that we need to collect only six more of them to summon the Colossus of Ultimate Destruction! So c'mon . . . we gotta strike while the iron's hot."

▶ ▶ ▶ ▶ ▶

Just outside the capitol city of Knightonia, the knights' Fortrex sat beyond the castle's main gate. Axl, Aaron, and Lance grunted as they worked together to push the solid granite statue of Clay onto one of the towers above the Bowtrex.

Macy gave her fellow knights a thumbs-up, calling out, "Perfect!"

"Why, exactly, did we have to move Clay to the *very* top of the Fortrex?" Axl asked, wiping sweat off his enormous brow.

"You heard Merlok," Macy said. "We have to treat him like he's still here. And I think he needed some fresh air."

Lance knocked his fist against Clay's stone head. "Hello? Super-Knight? You still in there?" He shrugged and said to Macy, "I don't think he cares where he is."

Just then, Merlok appeared on the view shield at the front of the Fortrex. "Oh my, yes," he announced. "Macy is correct. We must treat Clay like he is still a member of the team. As a symbol of inspiration, motivation, and support."

Lance rolled his eyes. "Yeah, well, what if somebody sees him up here, being all rock-i-fied?"

Aaron answered, "We simply tell them that the king commissioned a statue of Clay to honor him for saving the queen."

"Good thinking, Aaron," said Macy. "Right, Merlok? Merlok?"

But Merlok had disappeared from the view screen. Moments later, the bright orange hologram reappeared in the Fortrex workshop. "Robin, my boy . . ." Merlok 2.0 said, casting a glance at the Mech that Robin was repairing.

"Hey, Merlok," Robin said, pushing his welding helmet away from his face. "What's up? I'm just upgrading my Mech to Battle Suit tech, since it was so heavily damaged when the Cloud of Monstrox blew your library up again."

"Robin, I need you to work on a super-secret secret project for me," Merlok said seriously. "I will download some plans to your tablet, but you mustn't tell anyone else about it. Not yet."

"I like the sound of that," Robin said happily. "Whatever you need."

▶ ▶ ▶ ▶ ▶

Elsewhere in the Realm, Jestro and the Cloud of Monstrox were eager to try out their newest Forbidden Power. "Welcome to Bravington," the Cloud said to Jestro as it cast its shadow over the edge of the small town. "The *bravest* town in the Realm."

Jestro laughed evilly. "Oh, we'll see how brave they are . . ." He jumped into his airhead speeder (the Hatattacka) and raced into the center of the village, holding his staff at the ready. An army of Stone Monsters chased after Jestro, ready to do their worst. "Let's tear this scaredy-cat little burg apart!"

▶ ▶ ▶ ▶ ▶

Back at the Fortrex, alarms blared in the rolling castle.

"Knights!" Ava cried. "We've picked up another

Forbidden Power reading: Jestro's attacking the town of Bravington. The Fortrex is still having power issues, so we won't get there fast enough."

"Right, Ava," Aaron replied. He lowered the drawbridge and all five of the knights' vehicles blasted out of the castle. "We'll get there and hold off the monsters until you can bring the Fortrex into the fight!"

The four knights raced toward Bravington. When Aaron, Axl, Macy, and Lance arrived, they found Jestro, the Cloud of Monstrox, and their stone army terrorizing the people in the town. Overcome with fear from the Forbidden Power, the residents screamed and hid.

"That's right," Jestro cackled. "You better be scared of me!"

Just as Jestro was really getting into things, the knights swarmed around him. Aaron noted, "It looks like we're gonna end this fight before Jestro gets a chance to . . ."

But before Aaron could finish his thought, Jestro held his staff up and screamed, "Be a bunch of total CHICKENS!"

The blast of the Forbidden Power hit Lance full on and he whimpered, ". . . suck all the courage from my body and mind?!"

Macy raced toward her teammate. "Lance, are you okay?"

Lance curled up in a ball and sobbed, "I want my blanky. Or maybe I'll just suck my thumb . . ."

"Stay away from the beam of that Forbidden Power!" Aaron shouted as he fired energy blasts at Jestro. "It's freaking everyone out."

"We can't let those Blecho-Knights get organized," the Cloud of Monstrox boomed at Jestro. "Hit 'em with everything we got."

Monsters surged toward the knights as Jestro raced to turn the Forbidden Power on each of the knights.

"Quick, you guys—scatter!" Aaron dodged out of

harm's way as a blast narrowly missed him. Through his communicator, Aaron asked, "Ava, what's your status? We're gonna need a Combo NEXO Power to deal with this frightening situation!"

Ava's voice rang out, "We're just coming up on Bravington now. But I don't know if we have enough M.I.—'Merlok Integration'—to run up the Combo NEXO Triangulator."

Merlok's voice assured her, "We must risk it, my child. I sense that the Forbidden Power that Jestro is using is very, very frightening indeed."

Lance, who was still suffering the effects of the spooky Forbidden Power, cried, "I'm running off to find a juice box and a warm hug!"

Axl grunted, "I think we lost Lance."

"We gotta protect him!" Aaron ordered.

Lance whispered, "Oh, Mommy, we can hide under the bed. It's a good spot."

"Snap out of it, Lance," Macy said. "We're not hiding. And I'm not your mommy."

As a hulking army of Gargoyles charged at the knights, Aaron yelled, "Ava! We need the Combo NEXO Power—and fast!"

Ava was doubtful. She worried about what could go wrong if their system wasn't yet ready for this kind of power surge. But Merlok assured her, "We must risk it, my child. Prepare for Combo NEXO Power Scan!"

The Triangulator began to spin and whir. Macy looked at Lance, who was still shaking on the ground. "Lance, they're gonna need you for the Combo NEXO Power. Are you okay?"

Lance nodded slightly. "Yes, I'm feeling better. That is one scary Forbidden Power. Seems to wear off pretty fast, though."

Macy grabbed Lance and dragged him to where Aaron and Axl were already waiting. She provided cover as the three guys called out, "NEXOOOO KNIGHTS heroes . . . unite!"

Merlok's voice rang out, "Combo NEXO Power

Download: Raging Rally, Hammer Slam, Broom of Doom!"

With their new powers in place, the NEXO KNIGHTS team raced toward Jestro's monsters. Within moments, they were turning the whole rocky crew into rubble.

"No!" Jestro wailed. "Stop it! Oh, I'll make you too scared to use your power!" He turned his staff on the knights. But it had no effect on them because of their Combo NEXO Power. Helplessly, Jestro turned toward the Cloud of Monstrox. "What are we gonna do?"

The Cloud of Monstrox considered for a moment. "We need a monster they can't destroy . . ." Just then, he spotted the granite statue of Clay atop the Fortrex tower—and it gave him a very good idea. Just as the Cloud struck the Clay statue with a blast of its magical lightning, it cackled, "I've got an evil plan!"

CONCLUSION

What will become of Clay . . . and can Aaron step up to lead the knights?

What kind of secret project is Robin working on with Merlok?

Will Jestro and Monstrox find the rest of the Forbidden Powers . . . or will the knights be able to stop them before it's too late?

What kind of mayhem and monsters are in store for the NEXO KNIGHTS heroes as they continue on their quest to save the Realm from evil? Only time will tell . . .